25
ESSENTIALS

TECHNIQUES FOR
PLANKING

25
ESSENTIALS

TECHNIQUES FOR
PLANKING

The Harvard Common Press
Boston, Massachusetts

The Harvard Common Press
535 Albany Street, Boston, Massachusetts 02118
www.harvardcommonpress.com

Printed in China
Printed on acid-free paper

Library of Congress Cataloging-in-Publication Data
Adler, Karen.
    25 essentials. Techniques for Planking / Karen Adler and Judith Fertig.
        p. cm.
    Includes index.
    ISBN 978-1-55832-668-2 (case bound, spiral : alk. paper)
    1. Barbecue cookery. 2. Cookery (Smoked foods) I. Fertig, Judith M. II. Title. III. Title:
Twenty-five essentials, techniques for planking. IV. Techniques for planking. V. Title: Planking.
    TX840.B3A3177 2010
    641.5'784--dc22
                                                                    2009032139

Special bulk-order discounts are available on this and other Harvard Common Press books. Companies and organizations may purchase books for premiums or resale, or may arrange a custom edition, by contacting the Marketing Director at the address above.

Book design by Elizabeth Van Itallie
Photography by Joyce Oudkerk Pool
Food styling by Jen Straus with Jason Wheeler

We'd like to thank the good folks at Monterey Fish Market, whose beautiful seafood is highlighted in the photos in these pages. Contact http://www.montereyfish.com.

10 9 8 7 6 5 4 3 2 1

TO OUR FAMILIES,

who gather around the dinner table for special occasions

or just because

CONTENTS

STARTERS AND SIDES

FISH AND SHELLFISH

ACKNOWLEDGMENTS

FROM KAREN AND JUDITH:

Thanks to Ted Reader, who wrote *Sticks and Stones* and inspired us with his planked Brie; to Ronnie Shewchuk, who wrote a great book called *Planking Secrets* and has been a good barbecue comrade; to Mary Ann Duckers, whose sharp eye helps us with the editing; to Lisa Ekus, for her friendship and business acumen that help us through thick and thin; and to The Harvard Common Press, our publisher. Many thanks to all!

FROM KAREN:

Thanks to Judith, who cracks the whip and gets our projects done.

FROM JUDITH:

Thanks to Karen, who takes her time and then pulls some great material out of her hat at the last minute.

THE ESSENTIALS OF PLANKING

Planking is simple. You choose a hardwood plank and soak it in water for at least 1 hour before cooking. You place the food on the plank, place the plank on the grill or in the oven, close the lid or door, and cook.

What you get is food that is blistered, scorched, or browned, imbued with the gently aromatic flavor of the plank where the food has touched it. That means that, for the most flavor, we like to plank foods that are flat or have a large surface area to come into contact with the plank. Planked food is attractive, taking on a burnished appearance and a brownish-red color thanks to the smoke of the grill, especially from a charcoal fire.

Like any essentially simple technique, planking has developed sub-techniques. Here are the six basics:

1. *Indirect-heat planking* requires a fire on one side of the grill, and no fire on the other. You put the planked food on the no-fire side. If you have a fear of fire, then this kind of planking might be most appealing to you—along with oven-planking. Planking over indirect heat requires the most time on the plank as well, so foods pick up more aromatic flavor with this technique.

2. *Dual-heat planking* calls for a hot fire on one side of the grill and a lower fire on the other side; you put the plank on the lower-fire side. This is a hurry-up method for those who want to speed things along with salmon or chicken, for which the high-heat method might not produce the best results.

3. *Grill-planking* is done when you want to put grill marks on a food before planking indirectly. You already have an indirect fire, so it's a snap to grill a slice of eggplant, a breast of chicken, or a pork tenderloin on the direct side just until you have good grill marks. Then you simply put it on the plank and transfer it to the indirect side to finish cooking.

4. *Plank-roasting or high-heat planking* is used when you want to cook tender fruits, vegetables, or shellfish quickly and with more caramelized flavor. Place grilling planks directly over a hot fire (with a spray bottle of water handy). To plank-roast on an open brazier grill (one without a lid), simply tent a disposable aluminum pan over the planked food for the "grill lid."

5. *Smoke-planking* is planking with a kiss of smoke, and is great for foods that you would like to imbue with a little smoke flavor. Add wood chips to the fire, either thrown directly over hot charcoal or placed in a smoker box on a gas grill. Let the wood begin to smolder, then plank away. You'll get the aromatic wood flavor at the bottom of the food with a literal top note of smoke.

6. *Oven-planking* is ideal when the weather is just too bad to go outside, or maybe just because it's more convenient—for instance, if you plan to plank-roast. Oven-planking is usually done at around 350° to 400°F, while plank-roasting calls for oven temperatures of 450° to 500°F.

BUYING GRILLING AND BAKING PLANKS

Commercially packaged hardwood grilling planks are readily available in most towns and cities. Even if your town doesn't have a store that carries planks, you'll find thousands of online sources if you go to Google.com and search for "grilling planks." Planks can be reused until they're either too charred or too brittle to support the weight of the food.

Different shapes and sizes of planks abound, from the traditional rectangular grilling planks to crosscut ovals to thick baking planks. Individual-serving-size planks may be 4 to 6 inches square or smaller rectangular planks. The most common rectangular planks are 12 to 14 inches long and fit in most commercial grills. If you plan to use the planks in your oven, they can be a little longer, usually about 16 inches. So measure the length of your grill racks or oven racks to know what size plank will work for you. Plank thickness can vary as well; the thicker your plank, the longer it will last.

We also use 1½- to 2-inch-thick steel rod–reinforced baking planks (made for oven use, but also great on the grill), available at kitchen or barbecue and grill shops. The steel rod can be tightened to hold the wood together if it begins to split. These planks have a carved hollow that is perfect for keeping sauces or juices on the plank. Baking planks cost more than grilling planks, so you don't want to burn them up. Use them on the grill over indirect heat or in the oven at 350° to 450°F and they will last for several years. Food takes a little bit longer to cook on these thicker planks, which gives them more time to get infused with the wood flavor. In the recipes, we advise using a baking plank when food (like cherry tomatoes) might roll off a flat plank or a sauce will run off the sides of a flat plank, causing flare-ups and also loss of good sauce. For all of the other recipes, when we suggest grilling planks, baking planks may always be substituted. We just don't like to char the more expensive baking planks because then they do not last as long. An alternative is to set the baking plank on the grill atop heavy-duty aluminum foil to avoid direct contact with the flame.

If you want to buy wood for planking at the lumberyard, choose untreated pieces of hardwood. Do not use resinous wood like pine and fir or chemically treated wood, because resin and chemicals are not safe for consumption. We recommend untreated, seasoned alder, apple, hickory, maple, oak, pecan, walnut, and Western red or Northern white cedar, cut to the dimensions that best fit in your grill.

HARDWOODS FOR PLANKING

Barbecue stores and online retailers (including mainegrillingwoods.com, northwoodssmokeofmn.com, and cooking-planks.com) carry the largest variety of wood planks. Simply go to Google.com and search for the kind of wood you want, for example, "beechnut grilling planks" or "birch grilling planks." Also see the Resources (page 122) for additional plank vendors.

Here is a comprehensive list of the flavors and recommended uses of the many hardwoods available for planking:

- ALDER has a light, aromatic flavor that is great with fish.
- BEECHNUT is a mild wood that pairs well with both poultry and fish.
- BIRCH is similar in aroma to maple and is great for vegetables, poultry, and pork.
- CEDAR, either Western red cedar or Northern white cedar, is very aromatic and one of the most popular woods for planking, lending a deep but gentle woodsy flavor to foods of all kinds.
- FRUITWOODS like apple, cherry, peach, and pear are more delicate and thus perfect for planking fruit and seafood. Ham is also delicious on fruitwood planks.
- HICKORY lends a strong, hearty wood flavor to beef, pork, or poultry.
- MAPLE, oftentimes sugar maple, smolders to a sweet, mild flavor that pairs well with poultry, vegetables, or fish.
- OAK has a medium woodsy aroma that works well with any food.
- PECAN is a little milder than hickory and good for fruits and meats.
- WALNUT AND BLACK WALNUT are similar to oak, with a medium to hearty wood flavor that is especially good with tender wild game and red meats.

EQUIPMENT YOU'LL NEED

1. Hardwood grilling or baking planks that have been soaked in water for at least 1 hour.
2. A gas or charcoal grill, preferably with a lid, or an oven. If your grill doesn't have a lid, you can use an aluminum pan to make a tent over the food you are planking.
3. Heat-resistant mitts.

4. Two wide, long-handled spatulas for moving the plank onto the grill and then lifting it off the grill.

5. A pair of grill tongs for turning the hot planks.

6. A thermometer to gauge the internal temperature in your grill or oven.

7. A meat thermometer for gauging the internal temperature of the planked meat.

8. Wood chips, woody herb stalks, grapevines, and/or corncobs for smoke-planking.

9. A spray bottle of water to douse excessive flames.

10. A fire extinguisher for extreme emergencies (you should keep one in your house anyway).

11. A baking sheet for carrying the plank out to the grill and back to the dinner table or kitchen after cooking.

12. A wooden cutting board on which to set the hot plank while serving. Some stores sell serving holders to accompany planks.

13. A griddle made of heavy cast iron or cast aluminum for direct-heat planking. The plank sits on the griddle, which sits directly over the flame, thus preventing the plank from catching fire. This is especially desirable with the more expensive baking planks.

LET'S GET COOKING

Although placing food on a plank on the indirect side of the grill is the classic backyard planking method, there is no one definitive way to plank. Even the two of us like to plank differently. So, try a few of our planking recipes, and then develop your own signature style.

Whatever method you use, be sure to observe the number one rule: Never leave the grill unattended. The plank is made of wood and may catch on fire. (This goes for planking in the oven, too. Don't leave the oven unattended.)

THE FIRE

COVERED GAS GRILL. Depending on the recipe you are following, prepare an indirect fire (high or medium-high on one side, no heat on the other) or a dual-heat fire (high or medium-high on one side, low or medium on the other) in a gas grill with vertical burners. Horizontal burners work best if you turn on the burner closest to you and place the plank in the back of the grill.

COVERED CHARCOAL GRILL. For a dual-heat fire, mass two-thirds of the hot coals on one side of the grill and one-third of the hot coals on the other side. For an indirect fire, stack all the coals on one side of the grill and have no fire on the other side. Or, if you're using a long plank that fits better down the middle of your grill, consider center-planking: Bank hot coals on each side of the grill and have no fire down the center of the grill. The heat will be more even, but your plank may catch on fire more easily, so keep a spray bottle of water close by.

OPEN BRAZIER GRILL. The most common small brazier is a charcoal hibachi. Larger braziers on legs range from open kettledrum braziers to fancy catering braziers often called country club grills. If you want to plank on one of these, it can be done by tenting the planked food with an aluminum pan turned upside down to cover the plank and food. There is a greater chance of flare-ups, so have your water bottle ready.

OVEN. Plank in the center of a 350° to 500°F oven. Use a meat thermometer to gauge desired doneness.

THE PLANK

SOAKING THE PLANK. Submerge the plank in water for at least 1 hour, in either a wide, deep sink or a large rectangular plastic or stainless steel container. Use a couple of heavy cans from your pantry to weight the plank so that it stays submerged. After 30 minutes, turn the plank so it gets soaked evenly and will thus be more resistant to charring on the grill. Try adding apple juice or red or white wine to the soaking water—there will be a hint of flavor, but mostly the plank will just smell delicious.

SEASONING THE PLANK. Place the soaked plank over high heat for about 5 minutes. When the plank starts to char and pop, turn it over so the charred side is up, then arrange the food in one layer on the charred side of the plank. Or, to use a plank without seasoning it, arrange the food on the soaked plank and place it on the grill. Both methods produce great-tasting food, but keep in mind that you may want to season grilling planks but not baking planks (because they are more expensive).

ARRANGING THE FOOD ON THE PLANK. Food touching wood takes on wood flavor, so spread out your food in such a way that the maximum surface of each piece of food is in contact with the wood. Use two planks, if necessary, so you don't crowd the food. Then close the grill lid and cook to desired doneness. Each of the plank recipes in the book will tell you how long the cooking time is and how many planks you should use.

CLEANING THE PLANK. After you've cooked and served on the plank, clean it up with a little hot, soapy water and a good rinse. Do not soak the plank in soapy water or your next meal will taste like soap. Let the plank air-dry in an open, ventilated area. Eighty-grit sandpaper may also be used to remove any excess char after washing. Rinse the plank well after sanding.

After we've cleaned our planks, we use them again for any type of food. You don't need to worry that they'll retain the "Ghost of Planked Salmon Past" or hints of flavor from any other food you've cooked on them.

GRIDDLE-PLANKED BRIE WITH AMARETTO-PEACH CHUTNEY AND CRANBERRY CONSERVE

SERVES 8

Using a griddle—whether it is a built-in part of your gas grill (a common feature in an Australian-manufactured grill) or a heavy-duty griddle accessory—gives great results without burning your plank. It is our preferred way to use a thick baking plank on an outdoor grill, since baking planks are more expensive and we don't like to char them, so they will last longer. A baking plank has a carved hollow that will hold the warm, runny cheese spread with jam as diners cut into it.

An 8-ounce wheel of Brie or Camembert fits perfectly on a plank, but a 20-ounce wheel also works and is great for serving a crowd of 12 to 15 people. Larger wheels with greater circumference are too big to fit on a plank and will ooze out and make a mess all over the plank and grill, so stick with the smaller wheels.

Serve this with crusty French bread or crackers, if you like, and a chilled white wine.

SUGGESTED PLANK: 1 cedar or oak grilling or baking plank, soaked in water for at least 1 hour

PARMESAN AND CHEDDAR CHEESE BOARD WITH GRILLED GRAPES

SERVES 8

Hard cheeses like Parmesan and Romano are very easy to plank. They get nice and warm through and through and pick up a lovely hint of wood aroma. Cheddar is a bit softer and will melt ever so slightly with our directions below; it starts to melt before Parmesan or Romano. Other semi-soft cheeses like fontina and Swiss behave like cheddar on the plank, melting more quickly than the hard cheeses. We prefer wedges or blocks of cheeses and lay the largest surface of cheese on the plank, cut side down. A slightly lower temperature allows the cheese to absorb the wood flavor, but if you are in a hurry, you can crank up the heat. Use one large grilling plank or individual planks for each cheese. Grill both green and red grapes to accompany the planked cheese for a fabulous rustic appetizer. Arrange the planked cheeses on a large, attractive cutting board or a serving tray draped with a pretty kitchen towel. Serve this with crusty French bread or crackers, if you like, and a chilled white wine.

SUGGESTED PLANK: 1 cedar or oak grilling plank, soaked in water for at least 1 hour

INGREDIENTS

1 bunch seedless green grapes (about 1 pound)

1 bunch seedless red grapes (about 1 pound)

2 tablespoons olive oil

One 8-ounce wedge Parmesan or Romano cheese

One 8-ounce wedge cheddar cheese

1 French baguette, sliced, for serving

METHOD

1. Prepare an indirect fire in your grill, with a medium-hot fire on one side and no fire on the other.

2. Brush the grapes with the olive oil and set aside. Place the cheeses on the plank with the largest cut side of the wedges on the plank.

3. Place the plank on the no-heat side of the grill and close the lid. Plank for 15 to 20 minutes, or until the cheddar cheese is beginning to ooze. Remove the plank and grill the grapes directly on the medium-hot side of the grill, turning often, until the grapes are scorched and blistered, about 4 minutes total. Arrange the grapes beside the cheeses on a serving platter and serve with a basket of baguette slices.

OVEN-PLANKING: Preheat the oven to 325°F. Place the planked cheese in the middle of the oven and oven-plank for 15 minutes, or until the cheddar cheese is beginning to ooze. Serve with bread and fresh (uncooked) grapes.

PLANKED GOAT CHEESE WITH TAPENADE AND PRESERVES

SERVES 8

In plank-roasting, a grilling plank is set directly over a flame and can catch on fire. Have a spray bottle of water handy to lightly spritz the outer edges of the plank to hinder the flame. Part of the beauty and flavor of direct-heat planking comes from the charred look and taste that you get from the plank. Set the plank on a washable heatproof mat or a thick kitchen towel to avoid getting char on your table. This method is also great for planking firm cheeses like Gouda, Parmesan, or Romano, which taste lovely when warmed along with grilled fruits. So easy, but so good! Logs of goat cheese come in different sizes (4 ounces, 8 ounces, 12 ounces, and even larger), so if you can't find 8-ounce logs, substitute with the size you can find. Serve this with a variety of flatbreads, brushed with olive oil and grilled on the hot side of the grill before you plank the cheese.

SUGGESTED PLANK: 1 cedar or alder grilling plank, soaked in water for at least 1 hour

INGREDIENTS

Two 8-ounce logs fresh goat cheese

½ cup prepared olive tapenade

½ cup fruit preserves, such as cherry, fig, or apricot

Flatbreads or crackers for serving

METHOD

1. Prepare a medium fire in your grill.

2. Place the cheese logs on the plank. Spoon the tapenade over one log and the fruit preserves over the other log.

3. Place the plank directly over the fire and close the lid. Plank for 15 minutes, or until the cheese has a burnished appearance and has started to melt slightly. Serve immediately with bread or crackers.

OVEN-PLANKING: Preheat the oven to 400°F. Place the planked cheese in the middle of the oven and oven-plank for 15 minutes or until the cheese is slightly melted and everything is hot. Serve with crackers or bread.

PLANK-ROASTED PEARS WITH BLUE CHEESE

SERVES 4

Whether you serve these over dressed greens as a salad, on their own with a bold red wine as an appetizer, or as a sweet-savory dessert with a glass of port, you'll savor the extra flavor that plank-roasting over high heat gives this mild fruit. For plank-roasting, you'll scorch one side of the plank, then turn it over and place the fruit on the scorched side. The plank of fruit goes right over the fire in this recipe, so make sure you soak your plank for the full hour. Having a spray bottle of water handy is a good idea, too; just be careful not to douse the pears with water.

SUGGESTED PLANK: 2 cedar or alder grilling planks, soaked in water for at least 1 hour

INGREDIENTS

4 large, ripe Anjou or Bartlett pears

2 tablespoons unsalted butter, melted

2 tablespoons wildflower or other amber honey

½ cup crumbled blue cheese, such as Maytag or Point Reyes

Fresh thyme sprigs for garnish

NOTE: This recipe can easily be divided in half if you have a grill that is too small to accommodate two planks at the same time, or you can stagger the cooking.

METHOD

1. Prepare a hot fire in your grill.

2. Cut the pears in half lengthwise, leaving the stems intact. Using a sturdy teaspoon or a melon baller, remove the core from each half. Place the pear halves on a baking sheet, cut side up.

3. In a bowl, mix the melted butter and honey. Brush the honey mixture over the cut surface of the pears. Sprinkle the pears with the crumbled blue cheese.

4. Place the planks on the grill grate and close the lid. When the planks start to smoke and pop, after 3 to 5 minutes, open the lid and turn the planks over using grill tongs. Quickly place the pear halves on the planks, cut side up. Cover and plank-roast for 12 to 15 minutes, or until the pears are scorched around the edges. Garnish with thyme sprigs and serve.

OVEN-PLANKING: Preheat the oven to 450°F. Place the planked pears and cheese in the middle of the oven and plank-roast for 12 to 15 minutes, or until the pears are scorched around the edges.

PLANKED FIGS WITH PANCETTA AND GOAT CHEESE

SERVES 6 TO 8

Naturally sweet, fresh figs get an all-over taste treatment with tangy goat cheese, smoky pancetta, slightly bitter fruit liqueur, and heat from black pepper. Serve these figs as finger-food appetizers or place them on top of dressed greens for a salad. High-heat planking caramelizes the figs and burnishes the goat cheese, adding another level of flavor. The high heat cooks the fruit quickly, resulting in an outer charred fruit and warm center that has texture and bite but is not mushy. This is an excellent way to plank most fruits and vegetables. Keep a spray bottle of water handy to lightly douse flare-ups.

SUGGESTED PLANK: 2 maple or oak grilling planks, soaked in water for at least 1 hour

INGREDIENTS

½ cup crème de cassis or other not-too-sweet fruit liqueur, such as crème de mûre, or Calvados

1 tablespoon cracked black pepper

8 large, ripe black or green fresh figs, cut in half lengthwise, stems left intact

8 thin slices pancetta

1 cup crumbled fresh goat cheese

Clover or other amber honey for drizzling

NOTE: This recipe can easily be divided in half if you have a grill that is too small to accommodate two planks at the same time, or you can stagger the cooking.

METHOD

1. Pour the fruit liqueur into a shallow dish. Sprinkle the pepper on a saucer. Dip the cut sides of the figs first into the fruit liqueur, then into the pepper, and place, cut side up, on a baking sheet to marinate for 20 minutes.

2. Cut each slice of pancetta lengthwise into $\frac{1}{2}$-inch strips. Loosely wrap each fig half with a strip of pancetta. Fry the rest of the pancetta until crisp and crumbly and set aside.

3. Prepare a hot fire in your grill.

4. Place the planks on the grill grate and close the lid. When the planks start to smoke and pop, after 3 to 5 minutes, open the lid and turn the planks over using grill tongs. Quickly place the fig halves on the planks, cut side up. Sprinkle the goat cheese and fried pancetta on the figs. Cover and plank-roast for 12 to 15 minutes, or until the figs have softened and are scorched around the edges and the goat cheese has a burnished appearance and a brownish-red color. Drizzle with the honey and serve.

OVEN-PLANKING: Preheat the oven to 450°F. Place the planked pancetta-wrapped figs, sprinkled with goat cheese and fried pancetta, in the middle of the oven. Plank-roast for 12 to 15 minutes, or until the figs are scorched around the edges. Drizzle with honey and serve.

SMOKE-PLANKED STUFFED PEPPADEWS

SERVES 4 TO 6

We smoked these tasty tidbits in our book *BBQ Bash* (The Harvard Common Press, 2008), but they're also delicious smoke-planked! If you're having a party, you can grill another appetizer while you plank this one. Peppadews are slightly hot, slightly sweet miniature red peppers preserved in brine. You can find them in jars or in grocery store olive bars. We prefer using a baking plank with the concave center for the slightly rounded peppadews. The wonderful woody flavor that comes from planking is heightened with a wallop of wood smoke. It is easy to set up your grill with the wood for smoking as you are preparing the dish to plank, so it doesn't take any extra time. If you love the flavor, then add smoke whenever you plank.

SUGGESTED PLANK: 2 alder, cedar, or oak baking planks, soaked in water for at least 1 hour

SUGGESTED WOOD: Pecan, maple, or hickory chips

INGREDIENTS

16 brined peppadews, drained

4 ounces goat cheese

Olive oil for drizzling

Kosher or sea salt

Fresh rosemary leaves for garnish

NOTE: The little bit of smoke you get in the indoor oven dissipates quickly, especially if you close the oven door quickly after you remove the planked food. This recipe can easily be divided in half if you have a grill that is too small to accommodate two planks at the same time, or you can stagger the cooking.

METHOD

1. Prepare an indirect fire in your grill, with a hot fire on one side and no fire on the other. For a charcoal grill, soak 1 cup wood chips in water for at least 30 minutes and place directly on the hot coals when ready to plank. For a gas grill, place ½ cup dry wood chips in a smoker box (or wrap chips in aluminum foil and poke holes in the foil) and place over direct heat in the back of the grill.

2. Pat the peppadews dry with paper towels. With a small spoon, fill the peppadews with goat cheese. Arrange the stuffed peppadews on the planks and drizzle with olive oil. Season with salt.

3. When you see the first wisp of smoke, place the planks on the no-fire side of the grill. Close the lid and smoke-plank for 20 to 30 minutes, or until the peppadews are bronzed. Sprinkle fresh rosemary leaves over the top.

OVEN SMOKE-PLANKING: Preheat the oven to 400°F. Place ½ cup dry wood chips in a small metal pan on the bottom rack of the oven and let smolder for about 15 minutes before planking. Place the planked peppadews in the middle of the oven. Oven smoke-plank for 20 to 30 minutes, or until the peppadews are lightly browned and the cheese has a golden, burnished appearance and is warm and soft. Sprinkle fresh rosemary leaves over the top.

CHEESE- AND HERB- STUFFED PLANKED PORTOBELLO MUSHROOMS

SERVES 4 TO 6

The earthiness of mushrooms and the aromatic flavor of a wood plank are a match made in barbecue heaven. Most firm-textured mushrooms like button, cremini, baby bella, and portobello can be lightly tossed with extra-virgin olive oil, seasoned with salt and pepper, and placed on a plank to cook indoors or out. Small mushrooms that might roll around are better cooked on a baking plank with a carved hollow, or they can be sliced to lie flat on a grilling plank. Portobellos are also fine on a regular grilling plank. For this recipe, we've chosen the individual crosscut planks that are rimmed with tree bark and look great with the mushrooms. We also use direct high heat, so be sure to have a spray bottle of water handy to lightly douse flare-ups. Cut these stuffed mushrooms into wedges for finger-food appetizers, or make them the centerpiece of your meal, serving two per person.

SUGGESTED PLANK: 4 hickory, mesquite, or white cedar individual crosscut grilling planks, soaked in water for at least 1 hour

INGREDIENTS

4 large portobello mushrooms, stems removed

¼ cup extra-virgin olive oil

4 cloves garlic, minced

8 ounces crumbled or cubed feta, Boursin, Brie, blue, or goat cheese

2 tablespoons pine nuts, toasted

8 to 10 basil leaves, chopped

METHOD

1. Prepare a hot fire in your grill.

2. Place the mushrooms, gill side up, on individual grilling planks and drizzle each with 1 tablespoon olive oil. Into each mushroom cap, sprinkle one quarter of the minced garlic, crumbled cheese, toasted pine nuts, and chopped basil.

3. Place the planks on the grill grate over the fire and close the lid. After 2 or 3 minutes, check on the planks; have a spray bottle of water handy to lightly douse flames. Cover and plank-roast for another 5 or 6 minutes, or until the mushrooms are hot and the cheese has begun to melt.

4. Place the planks on dinner plates lined with napkins so they don't slide around.

OVEN-PLANKING: Preheat the oven to 400°F. Place the planked mushrooms in the middle of the oven. Oven-plank for 10 minutes, or until the mushrooms are hot and the cheese has begun to melt.

PLANKED RED AND YELLOW TOMATOES WITH FRIZZLED HERBS

SERVES 6 TO 8

Good grape tomatoes are now available year-round, and this recipe is a fine way to showcase them outside of a tossed salad. Serve these tomatoes with a simple grilled fish fillet, chicken breast, burger, or steak. The concave center of the baking plank will keep the tomatoes from rolling off.

SUGGESTED PLANK: 1 oak or cedar baking plank, soaked in water for at least 1 hour

INGREDIENTS

1 pint red grape tomatoes

1 pint yellow teardrop tomatoes

10 to 12 fresh herb sprigs, such as basil, oregano, marjoram, or flat-leaf parsley

½ cup grated Asiago, Pecorino Romano, or other hard grating cheese

Olive oil for drizzling

Kosher or sea salt and freshly ground black pepper

METHOD

1. Prepare an indirect fire in your grill, with a hot fire on one side and no fire on the other.

2. Arrange the tomatoes on the plank. Tuck the herbs around them and sprinkle the cheese on top. Drizzle with olive oil and season with salt and pepper.

3. Place the planks on the indirect side of the grill and close the lid. Plank for 15 to 20 minutes, or until the tomatoes have burst their skins and the herbs have frizzled.

OVEN-PLANKING: Preheat the oven to 400°F. Place the planked tomatoes in the middle of the oven and oven-plank for 15 to 20 minutes, or until lightly browned and hot.

CEDAR-PLANKED ROOT VEGETABLES

SERVES 4

Who knew that root vegetables could taste so good? Planking them results in a taste similar to that created in a wood-fired oven, only even more aromatic. Because root vegetables take longer to cook than less dense vegetables, we zap them in the microwave to parcook them. Other vegetables that look beautiful and would add another dimension of flavor to this dish are red potatoes, Yukon Gold potatoes, butternut squash, and carrots. Visual appeal is very important when cooking a medley of vegetables, so create your own sensational mixture.

SUGGESTED PLANK: 2 cedar or oak grilling planks, soaked in water for at least 1 hour

INGREDIENTS

1 large russet potato, peeled and quartered

1 large sweet potato, peeled and quartered

1 parsnip, peeled and cut into 2-inch pieces

1 large red onion, quartered

6 large cloves garlic, peeled

¼ cup olive oil

2 tablespoons chopped fresh rosemary

Kosher or sea salt and freshly ground black pepper

NOTE: This recipe can easily be divided in half if you have a grill that is too small to accommodate two planks at the same time, or you can stagger the cooking.

METHOD

1. Prepare an indirect fire in your grill, with a hot fire on one side and no fire on the other.

2. Prick the potato, sweet potato, and parsnip pieces all over with a paring knife and place them in a bowl. Microwave them on high power for 4 minutes. Add the onion and garlic, drizzle with the olive oil, and toss to blend. Stir in the rosemary and toss again. Season with salt and pepper and toss one more time. Spread the vegetables on the planks.

3. Place the planks on the indirect side of the grill and close the lid. Plank for 20 to 30 minutes, or until the parsnips have a burnished appearance and are tender when pierced with a fork. Serve hot.

OVEN-PLANKING: Preheat the oven to 400°F. Arrange the parcooked planked vegetables in the middle of the oven and oven-plank for 20 to 30 minutes, or until the vegetables are tender and lightly browned.

HIGH-HEAT PLANKED HADDOCK WITH LEMON ZEST TARTAR SAUCE

SERVES 4

Haddock with tartar sauce never tasted this good! Our easy-to-make tartar sauce is so much better than store-bought tartar sauce that once you try this, you'll be hooked forever. Haddock is somewhat delicate, so planking is a better technique for cooking this fish than grilling it. The high-heat technique for cooking is quite dramatic, and you'll need a spray bottle of water handy for dousing overzealous flames. If your plank catches on fire, the easiest way to control the flames is to move the plank to the indirect (no-heat) side of the grill and then lightly spray the outer edges of the plank with water. (But for heaven's sake, don't spray the fish!)

SUGGESTED PLANK: 1 cedar, hickory, or oak grilling plank, soaked in water for at least 1 hour

INGREDIENTS

Four 6-ounce haddock fillets

Lemon pepper

LEMON ZEST TARTAR SAUCE

1 cup mayonnaise

¼ cup sweet pickle relish

2 tablespoons grated onion

2 teaspoons fresh lemon zest

2 teaspoons fresh lemon juice

1 teaspoon Worcestershire sauce

Kosher salt and freshly ground black pepper to taste

METHOD

1. Prepare an indirect fire in your grill, with a hot fire on one side and no fire on the other. Have a spray bottle of water handy to douse flare-ups.

2. Place the haddock fillets on the plank and season with lemon pepper.

3. To make the tartar sauce, combine all the ingredients in a small bowl and stir to blend. Lightly spread some of the tartar sauce over each fillet, spreading it so that it seals the edges of the fish to the plank. Reserve the remaining tartar sauce for serving.

4. Place the planked haddock directly over the fire. Close the lid and cook for 5 minutes, or until the fish is opaque and begins to flake when tested with a fork. If the plank begins to catch fire, spray the edges of the wood with water. If the flames are considerable, move the plank to the indirect side and close the lid of the grill. The fire should subside.

5. Serve the fish with the reserved tartar sauce on the side.

OVEN-PLANKING: Preheat the oven to 400°F. Place the planked fish in the middle of the oven. Oven-plank for 10 to 15 minutes, or until the fish is opaque and begins to flake when tested with a fork. Serve with the reserved tartar sauce.

PLANKED GROUPER FILLETS WITH RED PEPPER-CITRUS BUTTER

SERVES 4

Individual serving planks are a unique and festive way to give each diner his or her own planked fish. The commonly available 6-inch square cedar planks are a perfect size for a single 4- to 6-ounce serving of fish. Individual thick-cut planks of untreated oak or maple can be found at the lumberyard, and specialty barbecue stores and online sources carry beautiful crosscut planks in flavors like mesquite, apple, beechnut, olive, cherry, and sugar maple. Individual planks are handled in the same way as the more common large planks, so if you want to do high-heat roasting or add a kiss of smoke, be our guest.

SUGGESTED PLANK: 4 individual cedar or alder grilling planks, soaked in water for at least 1 hour

INGREDIENTS

Four 6-ounce grouper fillets

Kosher salt and freshly ground black pepper

RED PEPPER–CITRUS BUTTER

½ cup (1 stick) unsalted butter, softened

Zest and juice of 1 lime

1 tablespoon chopped fresh cilantro

½ teaspoon ground cumin

½ teaspoon red pepper flakes

Kosher salt to taste

METHOD

1. Prepare an indirect fire in your grill, with a hot fire on one side and no fire on the other.

2. Place a grouper fillet on each plank and season with salt and pepper.

3. To make the butter, combine all the ingredients in a small bowl and stir to blend. Place a dollop of butter on each fillet. Reserve the remaining butter for serving.

4. Place the planked grouper directly over the fire for 3 or 4 minutes, until the planks begin to pop, then move the planks to the indirect side and close the lid. Plank for 15 to 20 minutes, or until the fish is opaque and begins to flake when tested with a fork.

5. Set each plank on a large plate and serve additional butter on the side.

OVEN-PLANKING: Preheat the oven to 350°F. Place the planked grouper in the middle of the oven. Oven-plank for 15 to 20 minutes, or until the fish is opaque and begins to flake when tested with a fork.

PLANKED SALMON WITH HERBED MUSTARD SLATHER

SERVES 4

Thick emulsified sauces are what a slather is all about. Mustard, mayonnaise, yogurt, and sour cream are all examples of ingredients that can be slathered on a boneless piece of meat or fish. Then the meat or fish may be baked, broiled, grilled, or planked. A simple slather can be used straight from the bottle, or you can adorn with seasonings or fresh herbs. The delicious fragrance of the herbs makes this dish sublime.

About center-planking: If your charcoal grill is large enough to bank the coals on either side, you can set the plank in the middle of the grill over no heat. Or, for a gas grill that has three vertical burners, turn the side burners on high and place the plank in the middle burner area over no heat. The fire on either side may lick the edges of the plank, so have a spray water bottle handy to lightly douse any flames on the plank. This is a very fast way to plank with the same amount of heat on each side of the food you are planking. Because the plank may catch fire, we prefer to use a grilling plank, not a baking plank.

SUGGESTED PLANK: 1 oak, cedar, or alder grilling plank, soaked in water for at least 1 hour

INGREDIENTS

HERBED MUSTARD SLATHER

$\frac{1}{2}$ cup Dijon mustard

$\frac{1}{2}$ cup mayonnaise

$\frac{1}{2}$ cup chopped fresh herbs, such as parsley, chives, and mint

Zest and juice of 1 lemon

One 1$\frac{1}{2}$-pound skinless salmon fillet

1 teaspoon olive oil

Kosher salt and freshly ground black pepper

NOTE: Slathers are great to use when timing (or attention span) is an issue. The slather keeps the fish moist even if it is cooked to well done. Good to know!

METHOD

1. Prepare an indirect fire in your grill, with a hot fire on each side of your grill and no fire in the middle. Have a spray bottle of water handy to douse flare-ups.

2. To make the slather, combine all the ingredients in a small bowl. Stir to blend.

3. Set the salmon fillet on the plank. Lightly coat the top of the salmon with olive oil and season with salt and pepper. Then brush the slather over the top of the fish, spreading it so that it seals the edges of the fish to the plank.

4. Place the planked salmon in the middle of the grill, where there's no heat, and close the lid. Cook for 20 to 25 minutes, or until the slather is a golden brown and the salmon is cooked through and flakes when tested with a fork. If the plank begins to catch fire, spray the edges of the wood with water.

OVEN-PLANKING: Preheat the oven to 400°F. Place the planked fish in the middle of the oven. Oven-plank for 20 to 25 minutes, or until the slather is a golden brown and the salmon is cooked through and flakes when tested with a fork.

PLANKED SWORDFISH OSCAR

SERVES 4

T his recipe has it all: ease of preparation, flavor, and eye appeal. The dual-heat planking technique is a hotter and faster cooking method, ideal for swordfish. Crabmeat is stirred into a mayonnaise-mustard mixture and then dolloped on top of the fresh swordfish, making it delicious and very moist. The asparagus gets a little bit of grill char, and all is well with the world!

SUGGESTED PLANK: 4 individual 6-inch square cedar grilling planks or crosscut planks, soaked in water for at least 1 hour

INGREDIENTS

Four 5- to 6-ounce swordfish fillets

$\frac{2}{3}$ cup mayonnaise

$\frac{1}{3}$ cup Dijon mustard

8 ounces good-quality canned crabmeat or lump crabmeat, picked over

1 clove garlic, minced

1 tablespoon fresh lemon juice

Kosher salt and freshly ground black pepper

12 thin spears asparagus, woody ends snapped off

METHOD

1. Prepare a dual-heat fire in your grill, with a hot fire on one side and a low fire on the other. Set a double sheet of aluminum foil over the low fire to protect the planks from burning.

2. Place a swordfish fillet on each plank.

3. In a small bowl, combine the mayonnaise, mustard, crabmeat, garlic, and lemon juice. Season with salt and pepper.

4. Grill the asparagus over the hot fire perpendicular to the grill grates, directly on the grill or on a grill rack, for 1 to 2 minutes. Place 3 grilled spears atop each swordfish fillet. Spread the crab mixture over each fillet, spreading it so that it seals the edges of the fish to the plank.

5. Place the planks over the hot fire for 3 to 4 minutes, or until the planks begin to pop. Move them to the low-heat side of the grill (atop the foil) and close the lid. Cook for 10 to 12 minutes, until the crab mixture is golden brown and the fish is just opaque and begins to flake when tested with a fork. (Have a spray bottle of water handy to douse flare-ups.)

6. Serve each individual plank atop a large plate.

OVEN-PLANKING: Preheat the oven to 400°F. Place the crabmeat-slathered planked fish in the middle of the oven. Oven-plank for 15 to 20 minutes, or until the crab mixture is golden brown and the swordfish is just opaque and begins to flake when tested with a fork. Serve with asparagus on the side.

SMOKE-PLANKED CATFISH WITH SUMMER CORN CONFETTI

SERVES 4

Farm-raised catfish fillets are firm enough for direct grilling but also do great on a plank. Catfish is mild and sweet and pairs well with any kind of salsa or aioli. The sweet, light smokiness of fruitwood is a good complement to the catfish, too. Fillets will smoke-plank much faster than a whole fish, so be careful not to overcook.

SUGGESTED PLANK: 1 pecan or oak grilling plank, soaked in water for at least 1 hour

SUGGESTED WOOD: Apple, peach, or pear chips

INGREDIENTS

SUMMER CORN CONFETTI

2 red bell peppers, seeded and chopped

2 ears fresh corn, kernels cut off the cob

1 bunch green onions, chopped

Kosher salt and freshly ground black pepper

Four 5- to 6-ounce catfish fillets

Lemon pepper

Olive oil for drizzling

Sprigs of fresh cilantro for garnish

Lemon wedges for garnish

METHOD

1. Prepare an indirect fire in your grill, with a hot fire on one side and no fire on the other. For a charcoal grill, soak 1 cup wood chips in water for at least 30 minutes and place directly on the hot coals when ready to plank. For a gas grill, place ½ cup dry wood chips in a smoker box (or wrap chips in aluminum foil and poke holes in the foil) and place over direct heat in the back of the grill.

2. To make the corn confetti, combine all the ingredients in a small bowl and stir to blend. Season with salt and pepper.

3. Sprinkle the catfish fillets with the lemon pepper and place on the plank. Spoon some corn confetti over each fillet and drizzle with some olive oil. Reserve the remaining corn confetti for serving.

4. Place the planked fish on the indirect side of the grill. Cover and smoke-plank the fish and vegetables for about 20 minutes. The fish is done when it is opaque and begins to flake when tested with a fork.

5. Serve the planked catfish with the additional corn confetti spooned over the top. Scatter the cilantro sprigs over all and give it a good squeeze of lemon juice. Garnish with the remaining lemon wedges.

OVEN SMOKE-PLANKING: Preheat the oven to 400°F. Place ½ cup dry wood chips in a small metal pan on the bottom rack of the oven and let smolder for about 15 minutes before planking. Place the planked fish and vegetables in the middle of the oven. Oven smoke-plank for about 20 minutes, or until the fish is opaque and begins to flake when tested with a fork. Garnish with the additional corn mixture, cilantro sprigs, and lemon wedges.

CEDAR-PLANKED CHAR WITH WOOD-GRILLED ONIONS

SERVES 4

Small whole fish like trout, char, walleye, bass, and even lake perch are excellent for planking, especially smoke-planking. They get the flavor of the wood plank on one side and a burnished golden color and smoky flavor on the other. An indirect fire is used to slowly cook the whole fish through. Char, in flavor and texture a cross between trout and salmon, is best planked whole. It's easier to fillet after it is cooked and stays moister that way. This method can be used with fish fillets and steaks, too. Whenever you grill fish, grill lemon halves alongside. The little bit of browning adds flavor, and the heat makes the lemons burst with juice.

SUGGESTED PLANK: 2 cedar grilling planks, soaked in water for at least 1 hour

SUGGESTED WOOD: Sugar maple or apple chips, or chopped corncobs

INGREDIENTS

4 whole Arctic char (about 1 pound each), cleaned

8 sprigs fresh tarragon

8 sprigs fresh dill

8 sprigs fresh flat-leaf parsley

8 stems fresh chives

Salt and freshly ground white pepper

Olive oil for brushing

4 lemons, halved

4 medium-size red onions, peeled and halved

NOTE: This recipe can easily be divided in half if you have a grill that is too small to accommodate two planks at the same time, or you can stagger the cooking.

METHOD

1. Prepare an indirect fire in your grill with a hot fire on one side and no fire on the other. For a charcoal grill, soak 1 cup wood chips or corncobs in water for at least 30 minutes and place directly on the hot coals when ready to plank. For a gas grill, place ½ cup dry wood chips or corncobs in a smoker box (or wrap chips in aluminum foil and poke holes in the foil) and place over direct heat in the back of the grill.

2. In the cavity of each fish, place 2 sprigs each of tarragon, dill, and parsley, and 2 stems of chives. Season with salt and pepper. Place 2 fish on each plank.

3. Brush the cut sides of the lemons and onions with olive oil.

4. When you see the first wisp of smoke, place the planks on the indirect side of the grill. Set the onion and lemon halves, cut side down, directly on the grate over the fire and close the lid.

5. Check the lemons after 2 or 3 minutes. If they have nice grill marks, remove them from the grill. The onions will take an additional 10 to 15 minutes and may be turned after the first 10 to 12 minutes. When they are nicely charred, remove them from the grill, too. Close the lid and continue to cook the fish until it is opaque and begins to flake when tested with a fork, 45 to 60 minutes total.

6. Fillet the char and serve on a platter with the lemon and onion halves.

OVEN SMOKE-PLANKING: Preheat the oven to 400°F. Place ½ cup dry wood chips or corncobs in a small metal pan on the bottom rack of the oven and let smolder for about 15 minutes before planking. Place the herb-stuffed planked fish in the middle of the oven. Oven smoke-plank for 45 to 60 minutes, or until the fish is opaque and begins to flake when tested with a fork. Garnish with lemon wedges. (Omit the onions.)

KISS-OF-SMOKE PLANKED SHRIMP WITH BÉARNAISE BUTTER

SERVES 4 TO 6

This is one of our most delicious and favorite recipes from *Fish & Shellfish, Grilled & Smoked* (The Harvard Common Press, 2002). The shrimp (or prawns, scallops, or lobster if you prefer) are napped with our wonderful béarnaise butter, with all the flavor of a classic béarnaise sauce—but it's no-cook! Just stir the ingredients together for a sublime compound butter or gently heat all of the butter ingredients to make a dipping sauce or a drizzle. Bread is a must for sopping everything up. The addition of smoke is a new twist to this recipe. Shellfish cooks more quickly than regular fish, so for maximum smokiness you need to get the smoke going in the grill or oven before you cook the planked shellfish.

SUGGESTED PLANK: 2 cedar or oak baking planks, soaked in water for at least 1 hour

SUGGESTED WOOD: Fruitwood chips, like orange or apple

INGREDIENTS

BÉARNAISE BUTTER

1 cup (2 sticks) unsalted butter, softened

¼ cup chopped fresh shallot

¼ cup chopped fresh tarragon

2 tablespoons white wine vinegar

½ teaspoon sea salt

1 teaspoon hot pepper sauce, or to taste

2 pounds extra-large shrimp, shelled and deveined

1 loaf crusty French or Italian bread

NOTE: This recipe can easily be divided in half if you have a grill that is too small to accommodate two planks at the same time, or you can stagger the cooking.

METHOD

1. To make the béarnaise butter, combine all the ingredients in a small bowl and stir to blend. Spoon the mixture into a ramekin or bowl and leave at room temperature for an hour or so before using. The butter can also be covered and refrigerated; bring it to room temperature prior to using.

2. Prepare an indirect fire in your grill, with a hot fire on one side and no fire on the other. For a charcoal fire, soak 1 cup wood chips in water for at least 30 minutes and place directly on the hot coals when ready to plank. For a gas grill, place ½ cup dry wood chips in a smoker box (or wrap chips in aluminum foil and poke holes in the foil) and place over direct heat in the back of the grill.

3. When the first wisps of smoke are visible, dollop 3 to 4 tablespoons of the béarnaise butter onto each plank and top with the shrimp. (Reserve the remaining béarnaise butter for serving.) Place the planks on the no-heat side of the grill. As the butter melts, toss the shrimp in it before closing the lid. Cook until the shrimp are firm and just opaque, 15 to 20 minutes.

4. Serve immediately on the planks with crusty bread and the remaining butter.

OVEN SMOKE-PLANKING: Preheat the oven to 400°F. Place ½ cup dry wood chips in a small metal pan on the bottom rack of the oven and let smolder for about 15 minutes before planking. When the smoke begins to fill the oven, place the planked shrimp with béarnaise butter in the middle of the oven and reduce the heat to 350°F. Oven-plank for 15 to 20 minutes, or until the shrimp are firm and just opaque. You may turn the shrimp halfway through the cooking to evenly coat with the butter.

PROSCIUTTO-WRAPPED PLANKED SEA SCALLOPS WITH FRESH HERB AIOLI

SERVES 4

With this technique you can use a grill griddle, or you can set aluminum foil over the low-heat side of the fire and place the planks on top of the foil; the foil (or the griddle) protects the planks from burning. These wrapped scallops look like little presents, and they are bursting with flavor and dolloped with fragrant herb aioli. Serve with grilled asparagus topped with some of the sauce.

SUGGESTED PLANK: 1 oak, maple, or cedar baking or grilling plank, soaked in water for at least 1 hour

INGREDIENTS

6 thin slices prosciutto

12 large sea scallops

Olive oil for brushing

1 loaf crusty bread wrapped in foil

FRESH HERB AIOLI

1 cup mayonnaise

¼ cup chopped fresh basil

2 tablespoons chopped fresh spearmint

1 tablespoon cracked black peppercorns

Zest and juice of 1 lemon

1 clove garlic, minced

Hot sauce to taste

4 sprigs fresh basil or mint, for garnish

METHOD

1. Prepare a dual-heat fire in your grill, with a hot fire on one side and a low fire on the other if you're using foil, or a hot fire on one side and a medium-low fire on the other if you're using a griddle. Set a double sheet of aluminum foil over the low-fire side and place the plank on top, or place the plank on top of the griddle over the medium-low fire side. Close the lid and let the plank heat for about 5 minutes.

2. Meanwhile, slice the prosciutto lengthwise and wrap each scallop with a half slice. Brush with a little olive oil and set them on the hot plank. Set the loaf of bread on the low-heat side of the grill, too, and close the lid. Cook for 15 to 20 minutes, or until the scallops are firm and just opaque.

3. Meanwhile, to make the aioli, combine all the ingredients in a small bowl and stir to blend.

4. Spoon ¼ cup of the aioli onto the center of 4 serving plates. Arrange 3 scallops around the sauce on each plate and garnish with a sprig of basil. Serve with the warm crusty bread.

OVEN-PLANKING: Preheat the oven to 400°F. Place the planked scallops and bread in the middle of the oven and reduce the heat to 350°F. Oven-plank for 15 to 20 minutes, or until the scallops are firm and just opaque.

HIGH-HEAT PLANKED CLAMS WITH DIJON BEURRE BLANC

SERVES 2 (OR 6 AS AN APPETIZER)

This mustardy beurre blanc is great with fish, seafood, poultry, and pork. The cornichons, tiny whole pickles usually served with pâté, add wonderful texture and taste. They are available in small jars at better grocery stores; check the olive bar if your store has one. This recipe is a bit complex, but the steps to make the sauce and parcook the clams are well worth the extra effort. The concave center of a baking plank is a wonderful holder for the clams, and the addition of smoke in the grill or oven is sublime. If you like, you can substitute mussels or small lobster tails for the clams.

SUGGESTED PLANK: 2 oak or cedar baking planks, soaked in water for at least 1 hour (see Note page 82)

SUGGESTED WOOD: Oak chips, chopped corncobs, or grapevines

INGREDIENTS

DIJON BEURRE BLANC

½ cup (1 stick) unsalted butter, softened

⅓ cup Dijon mustard

1 cup dry white wine

⅓ cup tarragon vinegar or white wine vinegar

1 shallot, minced

2 tablespoons minced fresh tarragon or 2 teaspoons dried tarragon

12 cornichons, drained and finely chopped

⅓ cup heavy cream

Kosher or sea salt and freshly ground black pepper

3 pounds clams (about 3 dozen)

2 cups chicken stock or broth

2 cloves garlic, minced

1 lemon, sliced

Loaf of crusty bread, for serving

METHOD

1. To make the beurre blanc, combine the softened butter and mustard in a small bowl. Cover and refrigerate for 15 minutes. In a small saucepan, combine the wine, vinegar, and shallot. Bring to a boil over high heat and reduce to ½ cup, about 10

minutes. Reduce the heat to low and whisk in 1 tablespoon of the butter mixture at a time, whisking between each addition, until all of the butter has been incorporated into the sauce. Whisk in the tarragon, cornichons, and heavy cream. Season with salt and pepper. Keep warm.

2. Prepare an indirect fire in your grill, with a hot fire on one side and no fire on the other. For a charcoal grill, soak 1 cup wood chips in water for at least 30 minutes and place directly on the hot coals when ready to plank. For a gas grill, place ½ cup dry wood chips in a smoker box (or wrap chips in aluminum foil and poke holes in the foil) and place in the back of the grill over direct heat.

3. Clean the clams under cold running water, scraping away the fibrous bits. Discard any with broken shells or shells that won't close. Set a large pot on the stove over high heat, and bring the chicken stock, garlic, and lemon slices to a boil. Add the clams, cover, and steam until they open, 8 to 10 minutes. With a skimmer or slotted spoon, remove the clams from the pot and place on the planks, discarding any that won't open.

4. Place the planks on the no-fire side of the grill and close the lid. Smoke until the clams have a smoky aroma, about 20 minutes. Place the bread on the no-fire side of the grill for the last 10 minutes of cooking.

5. Serve the clams with the warm beurre blanc and the bread.

OVEN SMOKE-PLANKING: Preheat the oven to 400°F. Place ½ cup dry wood chips in a small metal pan on the bottom rack of the oven and let smolder for about 15 minutes before planking. When the smoke begins to fill the oven, place the planked clams in the middle of the oven and reduce the heat to 350°F. Oven-plank for 15 minutes. Warm the bread in the oven during the last 10 minutes. Serve with the warm beurre blanc and the bread.

OAK-PLANKED CHICKEN CHARMOULA

SERVES 4

Planking chicken is gaining popularity right behind the traditional choices of fish and shellfish. Boneless, skinless chicken breasts (or thighs) are perfect for this recipe. The meat makes maximum contact with the plank, resulting in a wonderfully aromatic wood flavor. Charmoula is a Moroccan herb-and-spice blend that adds an aromatic depth to the chicken. It comes out beautifully burnished and flecked with the contrasting green herbs.

SUGGESTED PLANK: 1 oak grilling plank, soaked in water for at least 1 hour

INGREDIENTS

CHARMOULA

2 cloves garlic

2 tablespoons coarsely chopped fresh flat-leaf parsley

2 tablespoons coarsely chopped fresh cilantro

¼ cup fresh lemon juice

¼ cup olive oil

1 tablespoon ground cumin

1 tablespoon paprika

1 teaspoon kosher salt

½ teaspoon ground chile pepper, such as cayenne

Four 4- to 5-ounce boneless, skinless chicken breast halves or 8 chicken thighs

METHOD

1. To make the charmoula, combine the garlic, parsley, and cilantro in a food processor and blend. Add the rest of the ingredients and process until smooth.

2. Place the chicken breasts in a large shallow dish. Spread half of the charmoula over the top of the chicken, cover, and refrigerate for at least 1 hour or overnight. Cover and refrigerate the remaining charmoula until ready to use.

3. Prepare an indirect fire in your grill, with a hot fire on one side and no fire on the other.

4. Set the chicken breasts on the plank and place on the indirect side of the grill. Close the lid and plank until a meat thermometer inserted into the thickest part of the breast registers 160°F, 25 to 35 minutes. Serve with the remaining charmoula on the side.

OVEN-PLANKING: Preheat the oven to 400°F. Place the planked chicken in the middle of the oven. Lower the heat to 350°F and oven-plank for 25 to 35 minutes, or until a meat thermometer inserted into the thickest part of the breast registers 160°F.

PEPPER JACK-STUFFED CHICKEN BREASTS WITH CHIPOTLE-BACON SLATHER

SERVES 4

Boneless chicken breasts cook beautifully on planks. We incorporate four ways to flavor the chicken in this single recipe, and it is pretty easy, too. Stuffing them adds flavor and moisture, as does slathering them. The plank gives a nice woodsy flavor to the chicken, and the smoke adds the pièce de résistance! Canned chipotle chile peppers in adobo sauce are available in most large supermarkets—check the Hispanic foods section. The adobo sauce is very spicy, so use it sparingly if you decide to add a little to the slather. You could also make the glaze using half of a chile instead of a whole one; taste it, and if it's not too hot for your palate, then add the other half. The unused peppers and sauce can be refrigerated for several weeks or frozen for several months.

SUGGESTED PLANK: 1 apple, birch, oak, or cedar grilling plank, soaked in water for at least 1 hour

SUGGESTED WOOD: A combination of mesquite chips and apple or peach chips

INGREDIENTS

CHIPOTLE-BACON SLATHER

1 cup mayonnaise (low-fat is okay)

½ cup cooked crumbled bacon

¼ cup chopped green onion

1 chopped chipotle chile in adobo sauce, with additional sauce if desired

Four 4- to 5-ounce boneless, skinless chicken breast halves

8 slices pepper Jack cheese

METHOD

1. Prepare an indirect fire in your grill, with a hot fire on one side and no fire on the other. For a charcoal grill, soak 1 cup wood chips in water for at least 30 minutes and place directly on the hot coals when ready to plank. For a gas grill, place ½ cup dry wood chips in a smoker box (or wrap chips in aluminum foil and poke holes in the foil) and place over direct heat in the back of the grill.

2. To make the slather, combine all the ingredients in a medium-size bowl.

3. Cut a horizontal pocket into each chicken breast without cutting all the way through. Stuff each pocket with 2 slices of cheese, then place the chicken breasts on the plank. Spread each breast with the slather, making sure to spread it so as to seal the edges of the chicken to the plank.

4. Place the plank on the indirect side of the grill. Close the lid and cook until the glaze is golden brown and a meat thermometer inserted into the thickest part of the breast registers 160°F, 25 to 35 minutes.

5. Serve the chicken from the plank.

   OVEN SMOKE-PLANKING: Preheat the oven to 400°F. Place ½ cup dry wood chips in a small metal pan on the bottom rack of the oven and let smolder for about 15 minutes before planking. When the smoke begins to fill the oven, place the planked chicken in the middle of the oven. Lower the heat to 350°F and oven-plank for 25 to 35 minutes, or until a meat thermometer inserted into the thickest part of the breast registers 160°F.

PLANKED CHICKEN AMMOGLIO

SERVES 4 TO 6

This recipe was inspired by our dear friend Jean Tamburello, who served a delicious smoked chicken ammoglio at Marty's Barbecue, her former restaurant in Kansas City. Ammoglio is a classic Sicilian marinade that changes subtly from household to household, but it always contains olive oil, garlic, and lemon. Here a plank substitutes for the smoke and imparts a wonderful woodsy aroma and flavor to not only the chicken but also the ammoglio. The weight of the brick (use standard-size red house bricks) presses the chicken against the plank for even more contact.

SUGGESTED PLANK: 2 oak or cedar baking planks, soaked in water for at least 1 hour

SPECIAL EQUIPMENT: 2 bricks, wrapped in aluminum foil

INGREDIENTS

AMMOGLIO

½ cup extra-virgin olive oil

½ cup dry white wine

Zest and juice of 2 lemons

2 tablespoons chopped fresh flat-leaf parsley

2 tablespoons chopped fresh chives

¼ teaspoon red pepper flakes

½ teaspoon kosher salt

1 sprig fresh rosemary

1 chicken (3 to 4 pounds), halved, giblets and neck removed

2 or 3 sprigs rosemary, for garnish

1 loaf crusty Italian bread

NOTE: This recipe can easily be divided in half if you have a grill that is too small to accommodate two planks at the same time, or you can stagger the cooking. You could also plank one chicken half on the grill and the other in the oven at the same time.

METHOD

1. To make the ammoglio, combine all the ingredients in a medium bowl. Whisk well to emulsify. Pour half of the ammoglio into a large resealable plastic bag; place the chicken halves in the bag and seal. Refrigerate for 12 to 24 hours, turning once or twice. Cover the remaining ammoglio and refrigerate.

2. Prepare an indirect fire in your grill, with a hot fire on one side and no fire on the other.

3. Remove the chicken halves from the marinade and discard the used marinade. Place one chicken half, skin side up, on each of the planks. Rewhisk the refrigerated ammoglio and pour about ¼ cup over each chicken half. Let the rest of the reserved ammoglio sit on the counter to get to room temperature, about 30 minutes.

4. Place the planks on the indirect side of the grill. Weight the chicken halves down with the foil-wrapped bricks. Close the lid and cook until the chicken is opaque and a meat thermometer inserted into the thickest part of the thigh, not touching the bone, registers 165°F, 40 to 50 minutes.

5. Remove the bricks and set the chicken halves on a platter. Pour any juices collected in the baking plank's hollow over the chicken. Rewhisk the remaining ammoglio and drizzle it over the chicken. Garnish with rosemary sprigs and serve with the bread on the side for sopping up the delicious juices.

OVEN-PLANKING: Preheat the oven to 400°F. Place the planked chicken under the bricks in the middle of the oven. Lower the heat to 350°F and oven-plank for 40 to 50 minutes, or until a meat thermometer inserted into the thickest part of the thigh, not touching the bone, registers 165°F.

PROSCIUTTO-WRAPPED TURKEY BREAST ON CEDAR

SERVES 4

Wrapping a turkey breast in prosciutto makes a beautiful presentation, and it also helps to hold the cheese and herb stuffing in place. Since the turkey is wrapped with prosciutto, we prefer using the most aromatic of woods to penetrate to the turkey. A cedar baking plank is our choice for flavor, and the carved-out hollow holds any of the cheese that may ooze out while cooking. This recipe adapts well to chicken or pheasant breasts.

SUGGESTED PLANK: 1 cedar baking plank, soaked in water for at least 1 hour

INGREDIENTS

One 2-pound boneless, skinless turkey breast

4 or 5 thin slices Brie or Camembert cheese (about 1 ounce each)

5 or 6 fresh basil leaves

1 tablespoon capers

2 ounces sliced prosciutto

METHOD

1. Prepare an indirect fire in your grill, with a hot fire on one side and no fire on the other.

2. Make a deep slit lengthwise through the center of the turkey breast. Insert the slices of Brie evenly inside the pocket. Tuck the basil leaves on top of the cheese and sprinkle the capers into the pocket. Wrap the breast with the prosciutto slices and place it on the plank.

3. Place the plank on the indirect side of the grill. Close the lid and cook until the prosciutto is golden brown and a meat thermometer inserted into the thickest part of the meat registers 165°F, 1 to 1½ hours.

4. Remove from the grill. Tent with foil and let sit for 10 to 15 minutes, then slice and serve.

OVEN-PLANKING: Preheat the oven to 400°F. Place the planked turkey breast in the middle of the oven. Lower the heat to 350°F and oven-plank for 1 to 1½ hours, or until a meat thermometer inserted into the thickest part of the turkey registers 165°F.

PLANKED BEEF FILLETS WITH PORCINI SLATHER

SERVES 4

This is one of our favorite ways to plank meat, especially boneless steaks and chops. We grill one side of the meat to give it the direct flame and char that tastes and looks so good, then we slide the uncooked side of the steak directly onto the plank. The result is a great contrast in textures, with the seared crisp char on one side and the tender woodsiness on the other side. We also add smoke flavor to this recipe, but you can omit the smoke if you want. The porcini slather makes a little more than $^{3}/_{4}$ cup, and it will keep refrigerated for up to 1 week. You will need only half of it for this recipe, so save the rest to use another time on pork chops or chicken. It's also great as a dipping sauce for bread.

SUGGESTED PLANK: 1 cedar or oak grilling plank, soaked in water for at least 1 hour

SUGGESTED WOOD: Apple, oak, or pecan chips

INGREDIENTS

PORCINI SLATHER

¼ ounce dried porcini mushrooms, ground to a powder in a coffee grinder

¼ cup extra-virgin olive oil

2 tablespoons sugar

1 tablespoon kosher salt

½ tablespoon red pepper flakes

½ tablespoon coarse cracked black pepper

6 cloves garlic, minced

Four 5- to 6-ounce beef tenderloin steaks, cut ¾ inch thick

METHOD

1. To make the slather, combine all the ingredients in a small bowl and stir to blend well.

2. Prepare an indirect fire in your grill, with a hot fire on one side and no fire on the other. For a charcoal grill, soak 1 cup wood chips in water for at least 30 minutes and place directly on the hot coals when ready to plank. For a gas grill, place ½ cup dry wood chips in a smoker box (or wrap chips in aluminum foil and poke holes in the foil) and place over direct heat in the back of the grill.

3. Sear the steaks over the hot fire for 3 or 4 minutes on one side, and then place the steaks on the plank, uncooked side down. Top each fillet with about 1 tablespoon of the slather.

4. Place the plank on the indirect side of the grill. Close the lid and cook until a meat thermometer inserted into the thickest part of the steak registers 130°F for medium-rare, about 20 minutes.

OVEN SMOKE-PLANKING: Preheat the oven to 400°F. Place ½ cup dry wood chips in a small metal pan on the bottom rack of the oven and let smolder for about 15 minutes before planking. Meanwhile, in a medium-hot skillet, sear the tenderloin on all sides. When the smoke begins to fill the oven, place the seared steaks on the plank in the middle of the oven. Oven-plank for 20 minutes, or until a meat thermometer inserted into the thickest part of the steak registers about 130°F for medium-rare.

GARLIC AND ROSEMARY-SLATHERED PLANKED PORK CHOPS

SERVES 4

We prefer a baking plank for this recipe because the indentation on the plank will hold the olive oil slather, which would likely run off of a flat grilling plank and cause more flare-ups. The slather is delicious and is great for mopping up with crusty bread. You can use boneless or bone-in chops with this recipe. We chose boneless chops because they cook more evenly and quickly; simply allow more time if you choose to substitute bone-in chops. This recipe will work for any boneless meat chops, tenderloins, or poultry. Just cook to the desired doneness. For even doneness for denser meats like pork and beef, we like to turn the plank 180 degrees halfway through the cooking time.

SUGGESTED PLANK: 1 cedar or oak baking plank, soaked in water for at least 1 hour

INGREDIENTS

GARLIC AND ROSEMARY SLATHER

2 tablespoons extra-virgin olive oil

2 tablespoons mayonnaise

4 cloves garlic, minced

2 teaspoons chopped fresh rosemary

1 teaspoon kosher salt

1 teaspoon freshly ground black pepper

Four 1-inch-thick boneless pork chops (about 5 ounces each)

NOTE: Center-planking would work for this recipe, too. Then you wouldn't need to turn the plank 180 degrees halfway through the cooking. See page 64 for Center-Planking Fish with a Slather.

METHOD

1. Prepare an indirect fire in your grill, with a hot fire on one side and no fire on the other.

2. To make the slather, combine all the ingredients in a blender and pulse to blend.

3. Place the pork chops on the plank and slather the top and sides of chops, spreading the slather so that it seals the edges of the chops to the plank.

4. Place the plank on the indirect side of the grill. Close the lid and cook for 12 minutes. Turn the plank 180 degrees, close the lid again, and cook for another 12 minutes, or until a meat thermometer inserted into the thickest part of the chop registers about 140°F for medium.

OVEN-PLANKING: Preheat the oven to 400°F. Place the planked chops in the middle of the oven. Oven-plank for 20 to 25 minutes, or until a meat thermometer inserted into the thickest part of a chop registers about 140°F for medium.

INDOOR/OUTDOOR PLANKED BEEF TENDERLOIN WITH BUTTERED BRANDY BASTE

SERVES 6 TO 8

The trick to planking a larger cut of meat is to make it look good by searing the outer surface of the meat first and then placing it on the plank and completing the cooking process. If you are planning to plank outside, you can do the searing over a hot fire on the grill, or you can brown the tenderloin on all sides in a heavy skillet on the stove. This brandy baste adds color and flavor; it is so good that you'll want to eat it with a spoon. You don't want to lose any of this baste, so use a baking plank with a carved hollow to hold the precious liquid. You can also use pork tenderloin in this recipe; see the Note on page 118.

SUGGESTED PLANK: 1 cedar or oak baking plank, soaked in water for at least 1 hour

INGREDIENTS

BUTTERED BRANDY BASTE

¼ cup (½ stick) unsalted butter

¼ cup chopped green onion

⅔ cup brandy

2 tablespoons soy sauce

1 tablespoon Dijon mustard

Kosher salt and seasoned pepper

One 5- to 7-pound whole beef tenderloin

2 to 3 tablespoons extra-virgin olive oil

1½ tablespoons seasoned pepper

1½ tablespoons lemon pepper

Kosher salt

NOTE: Pork tenderloin can easily be substituted for the beef in this recipe. Two 1¼-pound tenderloins would fit on one plank and serve 6 people.

METHOD

1. To make the baste, melt the butter in a medium-size saucepan over medium heat, and sauté the green onion for 2 to 3 minutes. Add the brandy, soy sauce, and mustard and cook for about 5 minutes. Season with salt and seasoned pepper. Set aside.

2. Preheat the oven to 400°F. (Or, if planking outside, prepare an indirect fire in your grill, with a hot fire on one side and no fire on the other.)

3. Lightly brush the tenderloin with olive oil. Combine the seasoned pepper and lemon pepper and sprinkle over the tenderloin. Sprinkle salt over the tenderloin.

4. Heat a large skillet over medium-high heat on the stovetop. Sear the tenderloin on all four sides, 3 to 4 minutes per side. (Or, if cooking on the grill, place over the hot fire and grill for 3 to 4 minutes per side.) Set the tenderloin on the plank and spoon some of the baste over the top of the meat. Place the plank in the middle of the hot oven or on the indirect side of the grill. Close and cook for 20 minutes. Spoon some more of the baste over the meat, turn the plank 180 degrees, and continue to cook with oven door or grill lid closed until a meat thermometer inserted into the thickest part of the tenderloin registers about 130°F for medium-rare, about 20 minutes more.

5. Heat the remaining baste and spoon it over the planked tenderloin. Tent with foil and let rest for 5 to 10 minutes before carving.

MEASUREMENT EQUIVALENTS

LIQUID CONVERSIONS

U.S.	Metric
1 tsp	5 ml
1 tbs	15 ml
2 tbs	30 ml
3 tbs	45 ml
¼ cup	60 ml
⅓ cup	75 ml
⅓ cup + 1 tbs	90 ml
⅓ cup + 2 tbs	100 ml
½ cup	120 ml
⅔ cup	150 ml
¾ cup	180 ml
¾ cup + 2 tbs	200 ml
1 cup	240 ml
1 cup + 2 tbs	275 ml
1¼ cups	300 ml
1⅓ cups	325 ml
1½ cups	350 ml
1⅔ cups	375 ml
1¾ cups	400 ml
1¾ cups + 2 tbs	450 ml
2 cups (1 pint)	475 ml
2½ cups	600 ml
3 cups	720 ml
4 cups (1 quart)	945 ml
	(1,000 ml is 1 liter)

WEIGHT CONVERSIONS

U.S./U.K.	Metric
½ oz	14 g
1 oz	28 g
1½ oz	43 g
2 oz	57 g
2½ oz	71 g
3 oz	85 g
3½ oz	100 g
4 oz	113 g
5 oz	142 g
6 oz	170 g
7 oz	200 g
8 oz	227 g
9 oz	255 g
10 oz	284 g
11 oz	312 g
12 oz	340 g
13 oz	368 g
14 oz	400 g
15 oz	425 g
1 lb	454 g

OVEN TEMPERATURE CONVERSIONS

°F	Gas Mark	°C
250	½	120
275	1	140
300	2	150
325	3	165
350	4	180
375	5	190
400	6	200
425	7	220
450	8	230
475	9	240
500	10	260
550	Broil	290

NOTE: All conversions are approximate

RESOURCES

BARBECUE AND GRILL MANUFACTURERS

BIG GREEN EGG
3417 Lawrenceville Highway
Tucker, GA 30084-5802
(770) 934-5300
www.biggreenegg.com
Large producer of an egg-shaped, ceramic kamado combination smoker/grill that cooks at a higher temperature than traditional cookers.

CHAR-BROIL/W.C. BRADLEY
P.O. Box 1240
Columbus, GA 31902
(866) 239-6777
www.charbroil.com
Manufacturer of gas and electric grills and barbecue accessories. Also the maker of the New Braunfels heavy-gauge steel smokers and grills.

HASTY-BAKE
1313 S. Lewis Avenue
Tulsa, OK 74104
(800) 426-6836
www.hastybake.com
Manufacturer of the Hasty-Bake oven, a charcoal grill/smoker that has a crank system to raise and lower the grill grates over the fire. Side door for refueling is nifty, too.

KITCHENAID
P.O. Box 218
St. Joseph, MI 49085
(800) 422-1230
www.kitchenaid.com
Major appliance manufacturer of, among other products, outdoor cooking systems, refrigeration products, and refreshment systems.

VIKING RANGE CORPORATION
111 Front Street
Greenwood, MS 38930
(888) 845-4641
www.vikingrange.com
Manufacturer of stainless-steel gas grill outdoor kitchens and professional-quality appliances for the home.

WEBER-STEPHEN PRODUCTS COMPANY

200 East Daniels Road
Palatine, IL 60067-6266
(800) 446-1071
www.weber.com
Manufacturer of the original Weber grill since 1952. Grills, smokers, and all their accessories, as well as the Weber Smokey Mountain Cooker, a charcoal chimney starter, and more.

WOOD PRODUCTS AND PLANKS

BARBECUEWOOD.COM

P.O. Box 8163
Yakima, WA 98908
(800) 379-9663
www.barbecuewood.com
A variety of wood grilling and baking planks in alder, cherry, cedar, maple, white oak, and hickory. Also wood chunks and chips in hard-to-find varieties such as apricot, as well as all the usual woods used for smoking.

BBQR'S DELIGHT

P.O. Box 8727
1609 Celia Road
Pine Bluff, AR 71601
(877) 275-9591
www.bbqrsdelight.com
Compressed wood pellets for fuel and smoke in hickory, mesquite, pecan, apple, cherry, oak, black walnut, mulberry, orange, Jack Daniel's, sugar maple, and more.

CHIGGER CREEK PRODUCTS

4200 Highway D
Syracuse, MO 65354
(660) 298-3188
www.chiggercreekproducts.net
Hardwood lump charcoal, as well as a variety of woods: hickory, apple, cherry, pecan, grape, sugar maple, alder, oak, mesquite, peach, sassafras, persimmon, pear, apple-hickory and cherry-oak blends, in chips, chunks, and logs.

FIRE & FLAVOR

375 #B Commerce Boulevard
Bogart, GA 30622
(866) 728-8332
www.fireandflavor.com
Aromatic western red cedar grilling planks. Custom packing available.

NATURE'S CUISINE

#6 - 8444 Aitken Road
Chilliwack, BC
Canada V2R 3W8
(866) 977-5265
www.natures-cuisine.com
*Cedar, alder, and maple oven-roasting
planks. Wide variety of grill planks, too.*

WW WOOD

1799 Corgey Road
P.O. Box 398
Pleasanton, TX 78064
(830) 569-2501
www.woodinc.com
Smoking and grilling woods.

BARBECUE BOOKS, NEWSLETTERS, AND CLASSES

BBQ QUEENS

www.bbqqueens.com
*Official online site of the BBQ Queens,
Karen Adler and Judith Fertig. Features tips
and recipes for outdoor cooking, culinary
classes taught by the BBQ Queens, and
information about their books.*

KANSAS CITY BULLSHEET

Kansas City Barbeque Society
11514 Hickman Mills Drive
Kansas City, MO 64134
(800) 963-5227
www.kcbs.us
*Monthly newspaper published by the Kansas
City Barbeque Society, featuring everything
barbecue.*

NATIONAL BARBECUE NEWS

P.O. Box 981
Douglas, GA 31534-0981
(800) 385-0002
www.barbecuenews.com
*Monthly newspaper featuring barbecue
events and columns. Also the official newspaper of the National Barbecue Association.*

PIG OUT PUBLICATIONS, INC.

6005 Martway, Suite 107
Mission, KS 66202
(800) 877-3119
www.pigoutpublications.com
*BBQ Queen Karen Adler owns this company,
which offers more than 200 barbecue cookbooks.*

INDEX

ABOUT THE AUTHORS

KAREN ADLER and **JUDITH FERTIG** are the BBQ Queens and have been spreading the word on slow-smoked barbecue and hot-and-fast grilling throughout the country in magazine and newspaper articles, cooking classes, and television and radio guest appearances, and at special events. Karen has her M.B. (master of barbecue philosophy), Judith holds membership in the Order of the Magic Mop, and both have their Ph.B. (doctor of barbecue philosophy) degrees, all awarded by the Kansas City Barbeque Society's prestigious Greasehouse University, founded by Ardie A. Davis.

As cookbook authors, they've cumulatively written more than 20 cookbooks, including *Fish & Shellfish, Grilled & Smoked; Weeknight Grilling with the BBQ Queens;* and *BBQ Bash.* They have appeared on the Food Network's *Grill Gals* special and on PBS. They have been featured in *Food & Wine, Bon Appétit, Southern Living,* and many other publications. Both Queens are culinary instructors and have taught thousands of students the secrets of grilling, smoking, planking, and cooking fish and shellfish. Visit their website at www.bbqqueens.com.